Standing Tall A Memoir of Resilience

Ann Maharaj

In this deeply revealing, poignant, and ultimately uplifting memoir, She opens up about the harsh realities of her upbringing and shares intimate details of her life that only she truly understands

She had matching custom fitted pants, a staggering dark and silver coat, disco ball-formed diamanté studs, and misleading eyelashes on her eyelids that looked like cobwebs. A platinum blonde cropped wig, on the other hand, was the focal point. I gazed toward her head as she said, "It keeps my head warm." I squinted and

Jeanne, Barry, and I generally stayed inside the constraints of their lodge for their three-day stay.

pondered internally, "This is the most peculiar second in my life." Then I comprehended that I should have invited more people and perhaps set forth more energy. Jeanne, as anyone might expect, was apathetic about this. She seemed just as impressed by my two-year-old son's extensive collection of stuffed animals as she was by my newborn son discovering his tongue.

Prologue

She has been portrayed as capable of "heating up the fat from a taxidriver's neck" and "scratching the rust from the clothing rooftop," and her articulation has been described as "the nasal whimper of a Slopes Derrick needing a decent oiling." One author from The Australian portrayed talking her as similarly as 'holding

a conversation with a managing instrument', while another, from the

Sydney Morning Emissary, depicted her coarse tones as 'revolting,

elasticised vowels pushed up the nasal pit past a larynx

washed in Draino'. Jeanne says, "Ow, I really am revolting" was her reaction when she read these. She believes that the most delightful thing about her novel drone was that it was necessary.

The truth about Jeanne Little's voice is made clear, which is surprising. She was born on May 11, 1938, at the Crown Road Ladies' Emergency Clinic in Sydney (she will tell you in 1941, but as her partner Barry explains, "Don't all extraordinary stars fudge their age by about five years?"). the most youthful of seven kids who made due:

When my dad took me to the bar when I was a half-year-old to show off to his friends, they found a way to protect me from harm by grabbing me every time I left the bar, where he kept storing me between drinks. I didn't have as much karma returning home.

When Jeanne hit the footpath, her head split open "like a ripe watermelon." She was just a 16 ounces. From the accident, she still has a scar on her forehead.

Jeanne was rushed to The Randwick Young people's Crisis center

likewise, throughout the span of the accompanying two or three days, she encouraged a hack that

changed into diphtheria. The disease may cause paralysis and swelling in addition to permanent damage to the muscles of the throat, neck, and respiratory system. It affected Jeanne's voice pitch.

Due to this condition, I had a broad Australian accent, an inherited Scottish drawl (my mother's Scottish brogue was so thick that she used to call me

"Jin"), and God knows what else. I also had the worst voice in the world. It sounds funny to me. We all have burdens in life, and this is mine. Having said that, I have to admit that I usually speak clearly, probably because my mother was so hard of hearing. The analogy of the chicken and the egg is a common joke: Did my mother become deaf as a result of my shouting, or did she become deaf as a result of my shouting?

Jeanne was in the hospital for three months because she was so contagious. During that time, her family visited her from behind a clear screen and in white, sterile clothing. At the point when our younger sibling at last returned home, she didn't remember anybody of us, not even our mom," Cathie, Jeanne's sister, claims. According to Jeanne, nurse was her first word.

Jeanne's mishap was only another thing that Katie Mitchell, her mom, needed to do to part ways with her alcoholic spouse, Norman Landstrome. Katie had attempted to leave him once before, but her mother informed her that she needed to lie in her bed because she had made it. Jeanne explains:

After having two children, my mother asked my grandmother if she could escape this monster by returning to her parents' house until she could get her life in order.

But my grandmother denied. She knew nothing about how dreadful my rich mother's life was the point at which she had steady youngsters from a horrendous alcoholic.

At the age of 18, Katie Mitchell and her younger brother John set out for Australia from Glasgow, Scotland, in 1912. They moved there to see if it was a good place for the rest of the Mitchell family to settle after their father, John Spiers Mitchell, suggested that they check out "the land of opportunity." Shortly after the teens arrived in Sydney's main city, Katie started her own tailoring business in the CBD. Constantly speedy to make extra

cash, she also obtained private clients for sewing and fix

work around night time and on the finishes of the week.

Back in Glasgow, Katie worked to provide for her family. Her father had lost his job as a result of his involvement in union activities. According to Jeanne:

My granddad was the representative for a bread kitchen strike, and he was the main cook who got back to work after the strike finished. Because he spoke out, he was unable to find a new job, which caused my grandparents and their family a great deal of stress.

Without my mother's hard work, I don't know what they would have done.

Fortunately this money related fight was short lived. A year after Katie and John arrived in Sydney, they were reunited with their father, mother, and four siblings. Katie and John moved their family into a more modest, unattached bungalow in Waterloo in the wake of going out they had been living in Zetland. Jeanne's grandfather quickly found work as a restaurant janitor and elevator attendant at David Jones on Elizabeth Street.

To be sure, even as a young person Katie Mitchell had shown ensure, coarseness

besides, persistence. Jeanne describes her mother as "the driving force of my life." A feminist existed before the term was coined.' She was proficient in the fundamentals of business management and had creative and administrative skills. When Katie first met Norman, she was twenty years old, and everyone thought she was a pretty good match. She was logical, attractive, and determined. She had hired tenants to pay off three modest homes in Alexandria, a Sydney suburb, that she had put down as deposits.

Norman Daniel Landstrome, a well-known blacksmith from Warwick, Queensland, on the other hand, was 26 years old, had no responsibilities, and he was practically unemployed. After leaving behind his Swedish father, second-age Australian mother, and two sisters in Queensland, he had recently arrived in Sydney. The free-spirited Norman found country life to be too sleepy and yearned for opportunities in the big city.

Cathie, Jeanne's sister, says that her folks met at the Sydney City Mission, which was a spot for youngsters to meet and associate in its initial days.

My mother spent all of her spare time there. During a nighttime dance, my father happened to glance inside the Mission. In the wake of being welcomed into the lobby, he saw Katie and requested that she go along with him in the dance. After many more nights at the Mission, a relationship eventually developed.

Jeanne asserts that Norman was charming and attractive, extremely intelligent, and had a wicked sense of humor. My grandfather, her younger brother, and Uncle John were not pleased at all. However, my mother married my father after being seduced by his brash charms, despite their objections.

Katie and Norman tied the knot on January 8, 1915, at Chalmers Church on Chalmers Street in Surry Hills. About a year prior, they first met. At the point when serve Davey Brandt, a family companion, drove the Presbyterian function, it took on a more private feel. However, neither prayers nor blessings could save this relationship.

Unfortunately, Norman's wonderful family didn't prevent him from drinking. Truth be told, as the years went on, he got worse and turned out to be horrendously oppressive.

Soon, Norman's laziness and lack of direction became evident, and he spent money in the wrong places. Jeanne explains:

My father spent more than he could afford on drinks for himself, frequently for the entire bar.

He squandered the family's hard-earned money when my parents got married.

Jeanne's sister Lottie remembers going to Davey Brandt with her mother and younger brother Sandy shortly after the wedding.

There were no religious motives behind the visit; rather, it was for counseling with marriage.

The minister could be leaning on my mother's shoulder. He offered guidance on her marriage since it was obvious from the outset that there were issues between my folks. In those days, it was illegal to discuss a broken marriage with anyone, so many people, including my mother, sought assistance from the Church.

Katie had legitimate motivations to be vexed. Her husband had once rammed a carving knife through the kitchen wall a half-dozen times after hearing rats squeak, hunted down a cattle dog and shot it after it bit his daughter Cathie on the knee, and allowed a feral cat to roam free in the family home. "He said he won it in a raffle at the pub and laughed his head off as it hissed, spat, and tore the place up," Jeanne said. On another occasion, when Norman returned late from the bar, he moved into the lounge area, where the family table had been meticulously set up for a dinner party. Simply stunning was it. "My mother had spent hours ironing the linen tablecloth, shining her finest Glasgow china, preparing the food, and making it look beautiful like she always did," Jeanne recollects. Without saying a word, Norman tore the tablecloth from the table and smashed the expensive china into a thousand pieces.

As Lottie gets a handle on, her father's abuse was not physical

anyway, mental.

He never felt incited or incited. He just exploded.

Tension reigned in the air; As children, we were aware, so to speak, not to upset the apple cart, so we behaved ourselves.

Norman, according to Jeanne, has softer moments from time to time. She asserts that he shared moments of laughter with his children while cuddling in bed and was "strangely protective" of them. Jeanne knew, notwithstanding, that her mom profoundly despised Norman and faulted him for a ton of her distress, remembering the passing of her infant child John for 1919, in spite of these brief looks at delicacy. Jeanne explains:

My father insisted that John, my brother, attend the football game. He later died subsequent to getting the flu.

Katie in the long run chose to act, no matter what the outcomes.

Katie packed her belongings and her children into the car and drove away from the family's residence on President Avenue in Brighton-le-Sands, Sydney, on a Saturday morning in the early 1942, while her husband was, in Cathie's words, "in hospital on one of his many attempts to dry out." Jeanne had recently turned four. Two years earlier, Katie had purchased Belomena, a vintage weatherboard house at 21 General Holmes Drive in the same suburb. This property had all the earmarks of being a wise speculation, and she had an eye for property. When she moved her children into this house, she did not give her husband a forwarding address.

Jeanne explains:

Mother, she was astonishing. Before welfare and assistance,

she fled with her seven children. "A woman can do better than a man can," she always said. I can remember her always working so hard, carrying bags of vegetables home over her shoulder like a poor wharfe, taking care of us, and constantly cooking when she was truly such a creative woman.

At the same time, Katie articulated her independence and

set her family on another course. After years of living with a erratic, vengeful man, the family had finally found peace. Cathie, who was

thirteen years old by then, felt an extraordinary good inclination; He was abhorred by us. The family was aware that we might get by assuming that we left him. The beginning of a wonderful family life was marked by this. At long last, we were free.

Sister Lottie, Cathie's three-year-old sister, echoes this sentiment but adds:

My mom's choice to leave him didn't astound my dad at all. He'd been away an incredible arrangement

staying with his sisters regardless, endeavoring to get himself fixed.

He was aware that things had changed between him and my mother and that the family no longer accepted him. In point of fact, he was outside. We just let him go and never looked back.

Barry, Jeanne's husband, asserts, however, that despite the fact that the family may have left Norman that day in 1942, Norman's memory continues to play on the emotions of his children. He says:

I was sitting with all of the Mitchell children at a recent evening gathering. It was a large family get-together. They never stopped talking about Norman—what a beast he was, what he used to do, what he used to say, and how he treated their mother and them. They never stopped talking about Norman.

He has a significant impact on the lives of all of his children and causes them a great deal of emotional harm.

When Katie and Norman got married in 1915, they started a business that made ornamental ironwork. While Norman welded the multifaceted examples in a shed in the terrace, Katie made them on the kitchen table. Like most

of the spearheading attempts began by Katie, the

business was a reverberating accomplishment. The newlyweds opened businesses on Euston Road and Lawrence Street, respectively, in the Alexandria suburb of Sydney, as soon as it started to grow. Jeanne's sister Lottie recalled that "cows wandered freely" close to the new workplace her parents had established.

However, Norman quickly lost interest and, as is typical of him, wasted his time and money at the pub with his friends.

His two sons, Norman Jr. and Sandy, took over the business on his behalf. Katie applied for a new line of credit, purchased Norman's portion of the business, and gave him the former family home on President Road in Brighton-le-Sands and the plant on Lawrence Road when the marriage finally came to an end in 1942. She was quick to get rid of the financial burden of supporting her significant other. In any case, Norman, as per Jeanne, "felt that he had been given the crude part of a bargain thus he subtly set the production line ablaze while professing to be at Mt Victoria in the Blue Mountains, and guaranteed the protection for the property of £170," as Jeanne makes sense of. Norman was rarely fulfilled.

Be that as it may, Katie was not the last to catch wind of her flighty ex after this. Jeanne's niece, Faye Dunne, explains:

Norman was simply alluded to as "the elderly person" and never as "father" or "Norman" after he was removed from the family home. Katie would get furious letters from the "elderly person." He was, to put it simply, a nasty old drunk. The family would read his rants and ravings, laughing at the absurdity and discarding them.

After a lonely and bitter life, Norman Landstrome passed away in 1961, less than twenty years after his family had left him. Jeanne's sister Lottie states:

He passed away soon after my visit to Concord Hospital. My mom and my two siblings were with me. At the point when we showed up, he was oblivious. We as a whole fail to remember what turned out badly with him; I truly couldn't say whether it was heart inconvenience or something different. I had just come back from a trip abroad.

Only six people attended Norman's memorial service: his ex Katie, three of his kids, Lottie, Norman Jr., and Sandy, as well as Jeanne's uncle John and aunt Lottie, who mentioned the observable fact at that point, "Isn't it astounding that the six individuals who despised him the most are the ones who are here?" Jeanne was unable to attend. I actually don't remember why. She asserts, "I assume I was away."

Katie Mitchell made a lot of changes when she became single.

She changed the family name by deed poll from Mitchell, her maiden name, to Landstrome, her married name. Jeanne claims that she became a "blend of a mother and a father" after she changed.

The traits of a disciplinarian became apparent. Jeanne describes her mother as "generous but strict" and recalls, among other things, that she warned them before they went to Uncle John's house for afternoon tea:

"Try not to let me find you putting your hands up for more than one cake," she instructed.

Shortly after changing the name of her business, Katie moved into a new factory on Euston Road and renamed her family as The Mitchell Brothers Ironworkers.

Now, Katie and her hardworking sons created the decorative ironwork. Barry Little claims that Katie "treated like kings" and "left her daughters, though she loved them, to pick up the scraps." On famous buildings like the

University of Sydney's gates and the old Parliament House in Canberra, some of their best work is still visible. Other notable locations that once bore the Mitchell Brothers Ironworkers' stamp included the Callan Park Mental Asylum, the entrance to the Central Railway electric train station, department stores like Sydney Snow's, Anthony Hordern's, and the Hub, among others.

Then, close to the furthest limit of 1942, Jeanne was just four years of age, and the Australian government enrolled Katie Mitchell's child Norman to assist with ending the Japanese development three years after authoritatively announcing WWII. Her most young kid Sandy and ex Norman would oblige him a year sometime later. In Brighton-le-Sands, the sound of air strike alarms swirled around at home. The military set up shop in Cook Park, which had been the Mitchell children's weekend playground for a long time. Anti-aircraft guns, searchlights, air raid trenches, barbed wire, and a boom were commonplace along the Brighton-le-Sands beachfront. Also, barricade protections were introduced either side of the Cooks Waterway Extension on Broad Holmes Drive. Due to its proximity to Botany Bay and the Sydney airport, Brighton-le-Sands was particularly vulnerable to attack.

On the roads, the mood was gloomy. Streetlamps were reduced and shop windows were taped and barricaded to prevent their breaking in the event of an air strike.

To prevent aeronautical discovery, movie theaters were closed, games were stopped, and significant milestones were disguised.

If ladies, youngsters, the older, and the not well required to have been cleared to the nation, first guide stations were set up in quite a while and church lobbies.

Even though Sydney was well-prepared for an attack, its inhabitants were still shocked when it was invaded.

On the night of May 31, 1942, three Japanese midget submarines attacked the city before Norman Jr. was drafted. The invaders hid for several days in the Georges River, sank a ferry, and destroyed buildings in Rose

Bay before breaking through the defense barrier in Sydney Harbour.

Jeanne recalls, "When I was very young, I remember my mother walking along Brighton-le-Sands beach at night watching out for these Japanese submarines." She got the impression that she was helping Australia and the war.'

The frenzy that pervaded the Australian cognizance couldn't safeguard kids. Cathie, Margaret, and Elsie, Jeanne's sisters, began participating in daily air raid drills at the Brighton-le-Sands school. "a piece of rubber to bite on, two pieces of wood to hold on to, and two half tennis balls filled with cotton wool to protect their ears in the event of an air attack" were among the odd items in the students' school bags in addition to their lunch and homework, according to one historian. If they were to become isolated from their folks, some schoolchildren even wore a character circle with their name and address on it.

Others were relocated to towns in the western New South Ridges and the Blue Mountains. Not these safeguards were to no end.

Nearly a month after the Japanese submarine attack, a Japanese ship shelled Sydney, causing significant damage to Bondi, Bellevue Hill, and Woollahra.

Later, when Sandy and Norman Jr. were fighting, they often wrote to each other. According to Jeanne, their father was "contentedly eating bully beef stew out of his hat" "in the wilds of New Guinea" in one letter.

Katie Mitchell persevered: Despite the difficulties of living without a husband and the effects of war, she did not give in.

After her sons left to fight, she operated the ironwork business on her own. Katie's business kept on creating a gain in a space where most of Australians resided hand to mouth. Katie found time to redesign the family home in the midst of developing new plans for her ironwork, making adjustments to the records, and taking care of five children. Jeanne explains:

decisions regarding you as a possible love companion. They are subconsciously saying, "I want someone like me." Well, kind of like me."

If there is to be lifetime or even dating compatibility, there must be some degree of similarity. Our hearts work like finely tuned instruments to find people who share our values, beliefs, and worldview. Because it validates the choices we have made throughout our entire lives, comparability makes us feel great. We also look for people who enjoy the same activities so that we can have fun together. Indeed, similarity is a driving force behind successful relationships.

However, an excessive amount of closeness exhausts us. Additionally, we require someone to make up for our shortcomings.

If we don't have a head for math, who will check the books? If we are sloppy, who will pick up our socks?

As a result, we also look for characteristics in a long-term partner that complement one another. However, there are only qualities that interest us or improve our lives; there are no complementary qualities. Accordingly, we

search for a both relative and corresponding. person.

We'll talk about how to subconsciously instill feelings of similarity in your Quarry and demonstrate to him or her that, despite the fact that you have a lot in common, you are distinct in a lot of fun, useful, and interesting ways.

III. Equity: "Hey, baby, everyone has a market value! " is the "WIIFM" Love Principle. Everyone is worth something." How stunning is she?

How well-liked is he? How dim is her blood blue? How much impact does he have? Are they affluent, intelligent, and nice? How might they help me?

Is this terrible? As indicated by analysts, love isn't really visually impaired. Even the nicest people have a little bit of arrogance when it comes to choosing a life partner. Everybody asks, "WIIFM?" in the business world as well. What advantages do I have?

Some of you are disagreeing, and I can hear them saying, "No, affection is pure and humane." It encompasses compassion, charity, communion, and selflessness. Love is essentially that." Yes, that is the essence of genuine love between people who are good. You've probably even met couples who would do anything for one another and are deeply in love. Yes, there is the kind of unselfish love for which we all long. However, it appears on Page 12 much later. It just happens after you have prevailed upon your accomplice.

As per scientists, the most important phase in making somebody go gaga for you is to convince them that they are getting a reasonable plan. We may not know about it simultaneously, science tells us, dependable market

norms apply to appreciate associations. Unconsciously, lovers consider the relationship's cost-benefit ratio, the other person's comparable worth, the relationship's hidden costs, the maintenance fee, and the assumed depreciation. They then consider, "Is this all that offer I can get?" at that point. A huge scorecard is always in everyone's heart. In addition, if you want people to fall in love with you, you need to give the impression that they are getting a very good deal.

Is everything lost if you weren't born beautiful, if your grandfather wasn't Kennedy or Vanderbilt, or if you didn't have the compassion of a Dr. Schweitzer? No. In order to replace the silver spoon that was never given to us when we were born, we will, to some extent, investigate our verbal abilities. We can hence fulfill some extremely fussy Quarry.

IV. Inner self, What is Your opinion About Me? Allow Me To count the Manners in which Self image is at the actual heart of the primary heartfelt thunderings. Whenever Cupid focuses his small bolt at Quarries' souls, he could come up short. Science shows us where to really fire our weapons, right at their egos. People fall in love with people who make them look like their best selves.

Lovers ought to be overjoyed that ego makes the world turn because Quarries' egos are such simple prey. You can make your Quarry feel beautiful, powerful, attractive, charming, dynamic, or any other emotion you want. This can be done in a variety of ways. To cause your Quarry to feel extraordinary, there are enormous stroke praises, little-stroke touches, and a plenty of delectably wicked techniques. It is possible to get quarries to believe something they have always suspected: I'm different, and I'm great on page 13. As a token of my appreciation for your recognition of this amazing fact, I will fall in love with you.

Additionally, everyone desires security and approval. We look for protection from the cruel world in our primary relationship. The most effective method to Make Anybody Fall head over heels for You: Section Four ganders at how to cause your Quarry to feel like you are their salvation and a sanctuary from life's tempests.

V. Before the First Date, Gender Mapping Is There Love After Eden?

"Oh, why can't a woman be more like a man?" Rex Harrison moaned. from the 1956 Broadway stage, everyone smiled knowingly. He was aware that his Fair Lady came from a different species.

In contrast, feminists seriously questioned his beliefs in the years that followed My Fair Lady.

The envelope has been opened after many thoughts, assumptions, and hypotheses about whether people really differ in everything but their privates. "Yes!" is the response, please! Men and women think and communicate in completely different ways.

Neurosurgeons can distinguish groups of neurons in female minds that are answerable for men like Henry Higgins in My Fair Woman depicting ladies as "irritating, working out, unsettling, goading, and rankling."

The particles in the male cerebrum that make ladies blame people for being "unfeeling hunks" are the focal point of researchers' needles.

Despite the plethora of evidence pointing to the genetic, intellectual, and sexual differences between men and women, both hunters and huntresses continue to court each other in the manner in which they would like to be courted themselves. Even though recent scientific discoveries may help men and women learn more about each other's style, nothing short of a frontal lobotomy cannot permanently alter the kind of neurons that our brains produce. Women will continue

to be "bothering," and men will anyway be "unfeeling." Additionally, especially during first dates, both will continue to communicate in ways that distract from one another.

Serious major game trackers are familiar with all of the characteristics and propensities of deer, moose, caribou, buffalo, and wild hoards in an effort to frighten away their prey before they pack it. Likewise, serious love Trackers and Huntresses should know about the distinctions among people if they have any desire to kill somebody.

Part Five will teach you how to avoid the most common early-date turnoffs so that even the most cautious Quarry will feel more comfortable letting go of their guard. Love-tentative Quarry who generally take off

right when a man or woman gets unreasonably close will happily come very near your bolt.

VI. Rx for Sex

Directions to Turn on the Sexual Power

Many books on the most capable strategy to turn on your accessory make sex sound like flipping the switch on the night-light near your bed. " To accelerate your orgasm, click here. There, stroke for an extra expense." Sexuality is, in fact, electricity, even though your Quarry's bodily buttons merely accelerate or decelerate the physical functions. The strong machine runs on mindpower, which keeps it delivering heat for a long time. The cerebrum of your Quarry is the most sensual organ in their body.

There are numerous reference books that provide detailed instructions. "How to Satisfy a Woman Every Time and Have Her Beg for More," "How to Drive Your Man Even Wilder in Bed," and "How to Drive Your Woman Wild in Bed" are just a few of the titles that they carry. The list goes on. Such manuals are loaded with point by point data for women on the most capable strategy to invigorate that spot just

under the "enchanting little cap" to make him insane. Men can figure out where to let their hands walk so they don't miss the U-turn that takes them to her G-spot by looking at idiotproof charts.

All of this matters a lot, a lot a lot. Anyway, with respect to truly making somebody

fall head over heels for you, it neglects to compare what I'll call mind fellatio — sucking the dreams, the

longings, and the fantasies out of your

Page 15

Quarry, and a while later making a well established sexual radiation that the individual flourishes in.

Sensuality and passion in a relationship, gentlemen, are far more important to a woman than the number of times you can "do it" in a week or even a single night. Moreover, the emotions you express whenever you look at her. The size and shape of your sexual demeanor and how you manage his singular sexuality are definitely more important to a man than your bra cup size or hip bend.

No two sexual orientations are the same, like snowflakes. I will show you how to find your Quarry's novel sexuality and afterward give that person the adoration they need. We'll discuss the right sort of sex To some extent Six to make your specific Quarry go gaga for you.

Let's begin our six-part journey with the physical consequences of falling in love.

Page 17: "For what reason Do My Inner parts Go All Amusing?" is the real cost of falling head over heels in love.

Passionate feelings for someone are both a mental and physical cycle. Before their brains catch up, some of the first techniques you learn will set off your Quarry's physical response to you. We'll run a brain scan and x-ray on your Quarry to see what happens to him or her when they start feeling that amazing feeling called love.

"Does it require a pea-brain for someone to fall in love with me?"

In place of truth, yes. Scientists say that only people with PEA brains fall in love. They believe that a synthetic called phenylethylamine, or PEA, is at the core of fascination. It is a chemical cousin and has a "kick" that is similar to that of amphetamines.

PEA is created by emissions that cause a profound reaction practically identical to a medication high and travel through the sensory system and circulatory system. This chemical causes your hands to sweat, your internal organs to sweat, and your heart to palpitate. It is also said that PEA can make you want to rip off the clothes of your quarry as soon as possible.)

When we first experience the physical sensations of romantic love, the body produces phenylethylamine, dopamine, and norepinephrine, according to scientists. The body can get as close as it can to a natural high. When Cole Doorman sang, "I get a kick out of you," he was very clear about what he was singing about.)

The kick, sadly, does not last forever or even for very long. This adds to the rapidly expanding body of scientific evidence indicating that romantic love lasts only a short time. As a result, some people become "love junkies." Fortunately it really endures to the point of beginning incredible connections.

It typically lasts anywhere from one and a half to three years, which is plenty of time to build a wonderful relationship, win them over to marriage, or spread the species.

Now that you can't go around with a phenylethylamine-loaded needle, locate your Quarry, and inject the PEA-filled tube into their circulation system, you do the best thing you can. You figure out how to cause individuals to feel like they're becoming hopelessly enamored and get PEA-brained reactions in them.

"Why do we feel passionate feelings for one person, but not for another?"

People rarely suddenly and unpredictably experience a brain overdose of PEA and then develop a crush on the next person they see. No, the production of PEA and its siblings are initiated by emotional and visceral responses to a particular stimulus.

What kind? It very well may be the manner in which he welcomes her in an innocent way, the fragrance of her scent, or the delightful way she chuckles and kinks her nose. It's possible that the thing you're wearing is harmless and is driving your Quarry insane. For example, in 1924 Conrad Hilton, the trailblazer behind the Hilton

motel organization, flipped over a red cap that he spotted sitting five seats before him in house of prayer. After the services, he tied the knot with the woman who was walking underneath the Page 19 red hat.

"How Might These Little Things Begin an Adoration Relationship?"

Why does something so seemingly insignificant rekindle love? Where do they originate? Are they innate to us?

No, qualities have nothing to do with falling in love hopelessly. Because of the source, our minds are deeply buried. Our subconscious holds the ready-to-fire ammunition whenever we see, hear, smell, or feel something that appeals to us. It comes from what appears to be an endless well that gives us most of our personality— what we go through as children, particularly between the ages of five and eight. We experience a form of subconscious imprinting when we are very young, just like some animal species do.

In the 1930s, prominent Austrian ethologist Dr. Konrad Lorenz induced a flock of young ducks to form an unbreakable bond with him. Dr. observed how, shortly after hatching, ducklings begin to follow their mother in single file and continue to do so into adulthood.

Lorenz himself would imprint the ducklings.

Lorenz laid a clutch of duck eggs in an incubator. When he first noticed the eggs' tiny beaks piercing the shells, he squatted low like a mother duck and walked past them. They quickly got away from him and continued to follow him around the laboratory. From that point on, these engraved little ducklings continued to follow Dr. Lorenz on every conceivable occasion, despite the presence of genuine female ducks.

Specialists have exhibited that engraving doesn't simply happen in birds. In fish, guinea pigs, sheep, deer, buffalo, and other mammals, it can take many different forms. Are individuals immune to imprinting? We, then again, don't keep on following the specialist who conveyed us until we are grown-ups, dissimilar to the cheated ducklings who held up in line behind Dr. Lorenz. However, there is strong evidence to suggest that we are influenced by a different kind of earlier sexual imprinting.

The popular sexologist Dr. John Money coined the term "Lovemap" to describe this imprinting. Our Lovemaps, or carvings of pain or pleasure in our brains, are the result of our early responses to family members, childhood friends, and random encounters. Because the wounds are so deep, they remain in some part of the human mind for the rest of their lives, just waiting to bleed once more when the right thing happens.

Dr. Money said lovemaps. They are just as common as faces, brains, and bodies. We as a whole have one.

Without it, the species could not mate, fall in love, or reproduce. 7 There is a Lovemap in Your Quarry. Your Lovemap exists. We all own Lovemaps. They remain ingrained in our psyches, identities, egos, and subconscious forever. They may make a favorable impression. For example, perhaps your mom wore a particular perfume, your beloved dad smiled innocently, or your top teacher snorted with her nose scrunched up. When he was growing up in San Antonio, New Mexico, it's possible that a pretty woman in a red hat helped Little Connie Hilton.

Lovemaps can likewise be terrible. Women, it's possible that you were abused as children, which is why you can't love a man with a smug grin today. Men, it's possible that your cruel and wicked aunt wore

Joy perfume. Because of this, any woman who gives you a whiff of Joy makes you want to run away like an insect that has been sprayed with repellent.

Ways in lovemaps can in some cases be extremely muddled. Negative early experiences may cause them to take an odd turn. Women, you might be terrified if your date even glances at a passing woman because it's possible that your father left you and your mother alone with another woman. Gentlemen, despite the fact that your pretty babysitter spanked you when you were five, it was beneficial to your developing genitalia and stimulated them. As a result, unless a woman gives you love spankings, you can't fall in love with her now that you're an adult.

You may have forgotten about positive and negative sexual experiences, but your sexual subconscious can recall them. If someone sets one off when the time is right, BLAM! You receive a PEA injection through your veins. After it kills your brain and renders you unable to reason, you begin to fall in love. Sending off love is the significant glimmer.

That is only the beginning. The starter gets your vehicle rolling, and a short time later the battery overwhelms. Likewise, when your mind recuperates from its underlying PEA shot, a little explanation (ideally) starts to infiltrate the dark matter. As you get to know each other better, you and your PLP will start to talk about your similarities and differences (this is covered in Part Two), and you will both start to ask each other, "What can I get from this relationship?" Part Three). In Part 4, we pay attention to our ego and observe the amount of support it receives. Because early love is so fragile, we frequently turn off our Quarry by accident on our first dates (Part Five). Past that, what happens or doesn't unfold between the sheets assumes a critical part (Section Six). In How to Make Anybody Fall head over heels for You, we will examine every one of these viewpoints according to a logical viewpoint.

Right now, let's go back to the beginning. How are you supposed to find a romantic partner? How would you obtain the previously administered PEA to flow over you?

Section 4 of Page 23, Where Are All of the Good People?

"Where are all the good men?" is a question that young and old, single and divorced individuals across the United States are asking themselves. as they wake up, shave, put on makeup, brush their teeth, and touch up their gray hair. Where are all the beautiful women?

As per American Socioeconomics magazine, "one out of five Americans is single and looking. "8 This shows that 49 million Americans matured 25 and more seasoned are single, bereft, or separated. They are also getting bigger.

You respond, "Good, but if there are so many people around, where are all the potential love partners?" The response is, "They are everywhere, looking for love, just like you." PLPS include taking the commuter train, walking the dog, eating Blimpies in the park, listening to music at a concert, and eating at restaurants in your neighborhood.

Even with air travel, online dating, and a shrinking world, most people today marry close to home. According to studies on residential propinquity, as social scientists refer to it, Cupid's arrow does not travel far. In point of fact, one review reveals that the distance between a novice specialist and his Page 24 companion is only five blocks.9 Unless you've established your shelter in the Sahara, you won't need to travel far during your hunting campaign. With the strategies in this book, you can begin tracking Quarry close to where you are with new knowledge.

You've heard the moaning of darlings who fizzled: I'm looking for affection in every one of the places that shouldn't be there and in every one of the faces that shouldn't be there." The real issue lies somewhere else. The majority have failed miserably in their attempts to find love.

Performers in the performing arts are aware that getting cast in an audition requires a different set of skills than playing a role on stage. They must immediately utilize their talent to impress producers, sometimes in less than a minute. In addition, it takes a different set of skills to win someone over than it does to keep a long-term relationship warm. In some cases, you should knock your Quarry out in less than a minute. The person in question might in all likelihood never get to know you, not to mention experience passionate feelings for you, without that strong starting kick.

Page 25 5: Is it really love at first sight?

Imagine that you are lucky tomorrow and spot a potential love companion. The individual is roosted on the means

examining a book. or standing in front of a painting in a museum. or getting on a bus. or waiting in line to use an ATM from the bank.

You sneak a second glance. The stranger starts the internal PEA factory, and a small amount of it squirts through your veins. It could be the way he moves, what she's wearing, or how she looks. Her radiance? Is this overwhelmed with passion love? Is there such a thing as love at first sight?

Semantics are involved in that. There is definitely lust at first sight or instantaneous lust. On the other hand, the scientific community is pretty much in agreement that love at first sight is just quarterbacking on a Monday morning.

A successful love affair, possibly one that resulted in marriage, is regarded as true love in retrospect;

though when one is turned down, it is arranged as a fixation.

One fact remains in the absence of semantics in Clinical Parts of Human Sexuality 10. Love can be ignited by any immaterial occasion. When you realize a proverb's potential, the following are your first steps: In most cases, first impressions last. What else has changed?

These are brand-new: Even as we enter the 21st century, we still do not fully comprehend the significance of first impressions. Then again on what little nuances they are at times

based.

Gentlemen, a backward baseball cap or a gold chain flashing through your chest hair can make or break a new relationship before you even say "hi." Ladies can turn the handsome prince back into a scared frog when he says "hello" by turning one quarter of a turn away.

Always be prepared for affection!

Given the significance of first impressions and the possibility that a potential partner will make a "go/no go" decision as soon as they see you, the big question is: Why do people who are looking for love spend so little time taking their dogs to the veterinarian and so much time trying to look good on dates? Your Quarry will have a positive first impression of you once they know the date.

Naturally, being yourself on the date is important. However, it is nowhere near as conclusive as their initial brief glance at you.

Even though you don't know it, here's the awful truth: You probably let dozens of PLPS escape over the past few months because you weren't prepared for the kill and your trap wasn't set. That demonstrates, Trackers, that your clothing was not suitable. That indicates that you were not properly prepared, huntresses.

Clothing has a greater impact on first impressions for men,

according to research. It depicts a woman's body and face.

Huntresses, you might wonder, "Is makeup really that important?" the 31st page. Perhaps we should attend the examinations. Six different women, some of whom wore makeup and others did not, were given to men for conversation. In their review, "Lipstick as a Determiner of Initial feelings of Character," they found that when ladies wore lipstick, men had totally different assessments of them.12 Ladies, how frequently have you seen an attractive outsider without glancing toward you while walking around the road without cosmetics? If he is a typical man who draws attention to his pretty big eyes and rosy lips, what can you anticipate from him? Men, how many times have you attempted to converse with the Lovely Lady on the bus while wearing dirty clothes, only to receive a cursory response and be turned away? What do you anticipate from her, if she is a common woman attracted by a demeanor of skill and accomplishment?

First Method:

Men, you don't have to buy the newspaper in a three-piece suit to dress for "The Kill" everywhere. Ladies, this does not imply that you should apply three coats of mascara before walking the dog. It does imply that whenever you leave the house, you should prepare to kill. you and I.

Step out the entryway in an exceptional outfit. you and I.

The support hypothesis establishes us languid about first connections. Imagine that you are getting ready to kill someone. While acting as a traffic stopper, you go out three to four times to walk the dog, but nothing happens.

You declare, "Hey, this doesn't work." as a result.

In my seminars on sales, I tell people that most sales are made after the fifth call.

Give it time to function. You should never doubt that your future spouse will say, "Decent dog."

By name, who is he? Furthermore, what is yours?"

Page 32: Keep your mental doors open so that love can enter, in addition to being physically prepared. Stay psychologically "fit to kill." wherever you are. PLPS don't just hang out with singles at parties and clubs.

Cindy, a young and attractive manicurist, has been doing my nails for several years. It must contain a medication that causes women to break free of their restraints and spill everything about their lives as they clasp their hands across the nail trim table.) Cindy had griped to me for quite a long time that she just meets ladies in her profession.

I had a late appointment with Cindy one evening around six. After a long day of clipping, filing, and painting, she told me she's too tired to go to singles bars to try to meet someone. Around 6:45 p.m., a male voice in a deep voice said, "Excuse me, I know it's terribly late." The door opened behind Cindy's back. Regardless, is it possible to seek a nail treatment?"

After finishing Cindy's shoulder, I turned upward and saw a Greek god. I had no idea that these deities needed to be manicured! Cindy said, "No, we close in a short time," without actually pivoting, and before I could raise my jaw again.

"What are your thoughts on that?" She groaned as he left while focusing on my dangling nail.

When he arrives at this hour, "who does he think he is to expect a manicure?"

Then, outside her window, Cindy heard a Panther firing up. Her ears are extremely sensitive to high-end sports cars. Her Adonis was tilting out of the parking garage and out of her life forever in his smooth chariot when she got up to look. I respectfully suggested that people should always look for opportunities like this because she didn't stop cursing herself long enough.

Top salespeople never stop prospecting, whether they're at the dentist, copy shop, or pizza place. With another naked man he met in the Jacuzzi of his health club, a salesperson friend of mine won a substantial corporate insurance deal. According to the old song, "Find a million-dollar baby in a five-and-ten-cent store" is a possibility.

Technology No. 33, page 2:

Keep your mind "fit to kill" by setting bear traps before you even see the bear. Before the masses begin to swim in their direction, anglers set up their nets. The next big psychological trap probably won't escape if you set it as soon as you get out of bed in the morning.

Mentally and physically, you are now ready for love. "How might I make my Quarry's internal parts go all amusing when the person in question meets me?" is the next question.

Let's begin with two of the most potent weapons you really want to unleash on your love? They are in front of you right now. A common swear word is "I fell in love the moment I looked into my lover's eyes."

Page 35

7

Bit by bit guidelines to Light Unexplainable veneration

A man may be designated a chest man, a bum man, or a leg man. In addition, desplte the assertions of a few women, the majority of women are certified butt watchers. This is not just an idle guess: However, a British study that found these to be people's preferred eyeball destinations13 demonstrates that researchers have determined that everyone is an eye person. Exactly when you were a high schooler being

reluctantly or by and large familiar with pariahs, your people in all likelihood told you, "Gaze straight into

their eyes." After that, they would make it abundantly clear to you that you were not allowed to visit any of the anatomical locations listed above.

Forceful eye contact immediately elicits strong feelings of affection. This was conclusively demonstrated by a study titled

"The Effects of Mutual Gaze on Feelings of Romantic Love." 48 strangers, all 14 scientists, were grouped together in a large room. When having a casual conversation, they showed them how much eye contact they should keep with their partners.

From that point onward, the specialists examined every member concerning how they had an outlook on the different people with whom they had spoken.

What happened?

Page 36

Subjects who were taking a gander at their associate's eyes and whose accessory was thinking back definite

basically higher impressions of affection than subjects in another condition. . . . When the subjects looked at each other, their feelings of passionate love increased significantly. in addition to a love for their spouse.

Let's put it in a less technical way, Journal of Personality Research 15: When you look at the attractive stranger, it helps to put a match to the flame of love.

Why are eye contact's negative effects so severe? Helen Fisher, an anthropologist, claims that it is a fundamental instinct of animals. A crude piece of the human mind, calling forward one of two essential feelings — approach or retreat," is ignited by visually connecting. 16 A highly emotional state resembling fear is brought on by constant eye contact. The body produces synthetic compounds like phenylethylamine, or PEA, which shocks the feeling of being in love when you look at someone straight and forcefully. Therefore, making intense, almost threatening eye contact with your Quarry is one of the first things you can do to make them fall in love with you.

People immediately turn their attention away from sights they don't like when they see something they like. Our hands jerk up to keep our eyes from an awful movie scene, even though we enjoy spending long, lazy hours staring into a warm fire. It's the same when looking at other people. We avoid people who are unpleasant, unattractive, or boring despite our love for our partners. When we become bored, our eyes are the first part of our bodies to flee.

I'm acutely cognizant about this idiosyncrasy during my discussions. When I talk about a subject for too long, audience members bury their noses in their notes. It becomes even more crucial to examine their manicures. Some even doze off. When I get back on track, their eyes flutter upward like butterflies returning to the sun after a rainstorm.

Another factor that prevents good eye contact is the opposite of shyness. As they overwhelm us, we keep away from their eyes more and more. Representatives with exceptionally low positions much of the time try not to check the huge supervisor out. We will generally act similarly if we meet someone who is remarkably attractive, delightful, or successful.

I try to look everyone in the crowd in the eye when I teach. Nonetheless, at whatever point I spot an especially appealing man among the group, I regularly try not to check him out. I look into the eyes of everyone, with the exception of him. I force myself to look into the eyes of Very Attractive Male after realizing my error, and voila! My heart rate rises. I to a great extent lose my perspective. I mumble.

This eye contact has a lot of power.

How much eye-to-eye contact is required to copy Cherish?

An English scientist found that main 30 to 60% of when individuals are talking, they take a gander at one another. This is lacking to light sensations of head over heels love.

The well-known psychologist Zick Rubin first became interested in how to measure love while he was pursuing his graduate degree at the University of Michigan. The romantic young researcher later developed the first psychometrically based scale to measure the level of affection between couples at Brandeis and Harvard. It came to be known as Rubin's Scale, numerous social analysts actually use it to sort out how individuals feel about one another.

According to Zick Rubin's research on the "Measurement of Romantic Love," people who were deeply in love looked at each other a lot more when they were talking, and they took longer to look away when someone entered their world.17 He demonstrated this finding using a trick experiment. To assess the amount they cherished each other, he represented an extended series of inquiries to dating couples. " The waitress informed the couples, who were unaware of their ratings, that the experimenter would be with them shortly to begin the experiment. They were completely unaware that that was an experiment. Hidden cameras recorded the couples gazing into each other's eyes for an extended period of time. The couple invested more energy taking a gander at one another as their scores on the main test expanded. The less they loved one another, the less often they saw each other.

Make a lot more eye contact with your Quarry as you talk to give the impression that you are already in love—a self-fulfilling prophecy. Turn it up to at least 75% of the time if you want the PEA to flow through his or her veins.

The additional seconds spent communicating face-to-face speak volumes. "Beautiful lady, I am intrigued by you" will appear in the books. to a female I am awestruck by what you are saying. A man might interpret the increased eye contact as "I'm hungry for you." I am looking forward to seeing you fall in love with me and shed your clothes.

However, you must look into your Quarry's eyes directly if you want those feelings of love at first sight. Instead of focusing on his or her nose bridge, look directly into those baby blues, browns, grays, or greens. Envision that you are appreciating the optic nerve that runs behind the eyes.

"Whistle a happy tune, and you will be happy" is timeless advice from The King and I. In the same way, show your Quarry that you're in love with each other and they'll feel the love.

Third Method:

Make more than normal eye contact with your Quarry when you are speaking with them. In their body, look for the optic nerve. By locking eyes, you can give the impression that you and your Quarry are already in love.

Page 39 Notwithstanding, there is something else to it besides gazing eagerly at someone. You want to make your own eyes welcoming and inviting. Love is never really sparked by looking into the eyes of a dead fish.

How to Get Sexy "Bedroom Eyes" More than just movie stars have bedroom eyes. Clark Gable and Bette Davis lacked a patent on them. The intriguing look is imbucd in our transformative personalities for everybody. Ethnologists have even given it the name "copulatory gaze." In lovemaking, the copulatory look is vital. For example, before having sex, pygmy chimpanzees, which are about as human-like as an ape can get, spend a few moments staring deeply at each other.

For certain primates, having intercourse without eye to eye connection is troublesome. A number of Finnish researchers introduced male and female baboons to one another. Using blinder devices, they varied which part of the female's anatomy the male baboon first saw. Only five breaks occurred when the man's primary focus was on his woman love's intimate parts. Be that as it may, 21 discharges happened when he initially investigated her eyes prior to looking into her privates.18 (Men, expanding eye to eye connection during foreplay doesn't ensure 21 discharges, yet it surely energizes warm sentiments from your female.) " According to anthropologist Helen Fisher, "Maybe the eye—not the heart, genitals, or brain—is the initial organ of romance." 19 What is it about your eyes that draw people in so easily? Basically, huge students. In addition, assuming you see old photos of Clark Peak or Bette Davis, you will see that their students have fundamentally developed.

Most certainly a work of modifying, however hello!

The pioneer of the now-defunct field of study known as pupillometrics, Dr. Eckhard Hess, demonstrated to a group of men that women with large pupils were more appealing.

The main contrast between the two was that Hess had amplified the woman's understudies in one of the photos. A male response from Ms. Big Pupils was twice as strong as one from the same woman with small pupils. The trial was then turned around by Hess, who showed ladies pictures of men with bigger understudies. The female reaction to Mr. Enormous Understudies was also positive.

Although Dr. Hess informs us that we cannot deliberately control our student body, he demonstrated in the middle of the 1960s that we can essentially control it. Before connecting the male subjects to a Rube Goldberg apparatus to measure their pupil fluctuations, he presented them with a series of photographs. When they saw pictures of a landscape, a baby, or a family, the men's pupils slightly changed. Be that as it may, Hess slipped an image of a lady in her clothing into the heap. The men's eyes lit up when they saw that, indicating that when we look at an appealing stimulus, our pupils grow.

This is how to make your understudies appear to be welcoming pools in which your Quarry will actively drown. Just spotlight on the most alluring component on your Quarry's face while you two talk. Is that her adorable little nose? Is he smiling sweetly? Your understudies continuously grow as your eyes value the picture. Keep your focus away from that mole that has dark hair that has outgrown it. Your students will behave like snapdragons when they close their eyes as a result!

#4 TECHNOLOGY:

Suggestive looks While you are talking with your Quarry, center around the piece of their face that is generally interesting to you. Your pupils will automatically expand, so you'll get those bedroom eyes.

Also, think about loving thoughts. Concentrate on how lovely your quarry is, how agreeable you are with her, and how much fun it is to spend time with him.

Page 41 You should also get rid of doubt, anxiety, modesty, and any other negative understudy finishing thoughts. Think of your Quarry with warm, fuzzy thoughts to soften your gaze even more.

How to Make Your Quarry Feelings Primal, Terrifying, and Sexy Now let's talk about the third way to get your first organ of romance to feel primal, terrifying, and seductive. This one gives your Quarry that primal, uneasy feeling that comes with dating.

With the exception of when they are captivated by the audience (or utterly enamored), people will typically look away briefly at the conclusion of a sentence or during hushes. The expression "he couldn't take his eyes off her" is also a metaphor. Friends and family visually connect while talking, yet they additionally wonder whether or not to turn away from each other in any event, when they have gotten done with talking. It is destroying when someone's look looks out for you during the calm, after you've

quieted.

I employed a woodworker to add a window to my office quite a while prior. Jerry had relatively little physical or mental strength, yet oddly enough I thought that he is exceptionally alluring. Jerry had a mysterious quality that was hard to pin down. Unsettling, primal, and sexy, it was.

Nevertheless, I refused to indulge in my brief love affair. I might have thought that seducing the carpenter was neither politically correct nor desirable given the circumstances. On the other hand, maybe my Lovemap didn't show all of Jerry's different characteristics. However, Jerry took over my fantasies for weeks.

I hadn't seen him in some time. I also needed shelves to store my research materials while working on this book. I typically called Jerry. Three years older, ten pounds heavier, and just as sexy, he showed up at my door. This time, I understood the reason why he charmed me five minutes into our discussion because of my new exploration.

Page 42 Whenever I said something, Jerry's eyes stayed on mine. Even during the pauses after I finished speaking, his gaze remained fixed on mine. I realized how sexy, unsettling, and primordial that quality had been to me.

As our discussion of my shelves progressed, I also understood why Jerry was maintaining a longer eye contact. He never intended to be sexual. I wasn't interesting to him. He wasn't saying that he couldn't stop looking at me. Because Jerry wasn't very bright, it took me an extra beat to get my "I'd like the shelves eleven inches wide" into his head.

Now that we have this, we turn it into a way to boost your new PLP and rekindle those primal, frightful, and sexy feelings.

Technique No. 5:

Cheap EYES

Exactly when you are talking with your Quarry, let your

eyes stay adhered to his or hers to some degree longer — regardless, during

the calms.

Primitive, slightly unsettling feelings are elicited over time by a glance. It sets off something very similar "survival" synthetic substances that we experience when we are infatuated.

When you are forced to look away, resist. When you spot a lovely lady, what's the best procedure?

As if your eyes were encased in warm taffy, slowly draw them away. Give your body permission to speak for you. First, use your eyes. For a few more seconds, keep your eyes on her. Set yourself up for her to dismiss. At the point when a man takes a gander at a lady, she is educated to bring down her eyes. Actually, this does not imply that she is uninterested. If the woman looks up again within 45 seconds of looking away, she is requesting your attention, according to a study of flirtation patterns.

Set your chronograph, honorable men. As she coyly pretends to be interested in another object in the room, keep track of how long it takes for her to turn around and look back at you. Follow these steps if it happens in less than 45 scconds.

Give her a little gesture and a grin. It's like reserving a spot for a table at an opulent café. Once you have caught the attention of a woman, you have reserved the right to speak with her. Get rid of any and all concerns about "What will she think of me if I move too quickly or too forward?" In the event that you do not meet her, she will not care about you, fortunate or not. If you don't act quickly, every woman will flee from you.

Method #7, Planned FOR Trackers:

MOVE FAST "Move quickly" does not mean rushing toward your Quarry and slamming into her bones. Simply put, it means expressing your interest and immediately establishing your presence. This is the most tried approach.

Take a gander at one another. Maintain steady eye contact with her, but do not maintain it for an excessive amount of time.

Make fun of her. Ensure that your grin is cordial and conscious, not a pompous smile or a sneer that establishes a terrible connection.

Give her a compliment. If she looks back at you within the crucial 45 seconds, slightly nod. The nod reads, "I like you." Could we arrange a time to speak?

Turn your attention to her. The final step is to approach her sufficiently to speak with her.

You are now prepared for conversation. What should you first say to her? Delete the words in the opening line from your perspective. Customary lines go over a lot of that way — lines. "What's a good opening line?" has been a common question from shy Hunters. following seminars about my love. I find men contemplating such dilemmas charming.

Page 48 Once, a very reserved man who was attending my seminar took out a book called "How to Pick Up Girls" with pages that were dog-eared. It would appear that he wasn't the only one looking for this kind of advice. Since its publication 25 years ago, the book has sold more than two million copies, primarily through advertisements in men's magazines. Try not to let me know a delightful young lady as you doesn't have a date this evening" and "Would you say you are a model?" are two instances. When Father met Mother, this glimmering exchange might have worked; however, in our more illuminated times, ladies despise lines. The secret you look for and the method by which you communicate anything you say is unquestionably more important than what you say.

Gentlemen, your opening statements should be about the woman or the current circumstance. Ask her what

time it is. Do right by her watch or outfit. Get her to give you directions. Find out how she knows who is hosting the party. In fact, she is not processing your words at this early stage of your relationship; Instead, she is evaluating you, so the dumber your opening, the better. Her mind is hard at work assessing your words and demeanor. She is aware that anything you say is merely an excuse for speaking with her. If she likes you, that's fine with her.

You should pay attention to the first words you say, even though you shouldn't memorize any lines. Your first words should make her happy, just like your first appearance should make her happy. Keep in mind that everything in that first sentence to your Quarry is her sample of you up to this point. In her book, you will be viewed as a whiner on the off chance that you start with one. If you begin with an arrogant comment, she will label you as a braggart. However, if your first words charm her, she will find you charming.

Gentlemen, it's possible that you're wondering why you need to keep your cool. Why must your approach be so controlled, precise, and subtle? Nature returns to everything. Canvassed some place down in a woman's faculties, when she sees you, is a subconscious judgment of you as a possible accessory. She wants you to feel a sense of attraction toward her. But she also wants to know if you can control your lust for animals, which would show her that you would be a great partner.

Huntresses, Make the Fast Move . . . You might believe that the man is responsible for the pickup, First Huntresses. However, research reveals that two-thirds of all interactions are initiated by women.

This is also part of the grand scheme of nature. In the collective of animals, stepping the ground, hooting, or crowing are manners by which sweethearts to-be draw in each other. They stand out more than people. The female chimpanzee will "stroll up to the male, and tip her buttocks toward his nose to get his attention" when she spots a heathen chimpanzee. Then, at that point, she'll truly pull him up to his feet to have sex. " 20 This behavior is referred to as female proceptivity. Our species does not lack female proceptivity (in contrast to receptivity), even though we are, I should hope, a little less obvious.

How do women begin a romantic relationship? like what kids do. the same way that the brilliant creatures in God's realm, like birds, honey bees, and different bugs, do: with a gadget that gets people's attention.

Women, let's say you see Mr. Attractive More Bizarre huffing and puffing on the following StairMaster at the exercise center or at the disco across the table from you at the Senior Community. What should you do?

This is how the typical situation looks. A woman notices him and briefly looks at him before turning away. More brave women flash a small smile and then turn away, hoping that he will then step up to the plate (despite the fact that she would rather not come forward).

If this is your entire strategy, your chances of falling in love with Mr. Handsome Stranger may as well be one in fifty thousand, just like fifty thousand tiny seeds fall from a flower but only one takes root. Smiling and allowing nature to take care of the rest is not enough. More must be done than that.

Page 50: The Best First Steps for Women Let's examine the studies to find out what works. A researcher named Monica Moore was intrigued to learn how women carried out the two-thirds of the approaches. She recorded what are scientifically known as nonverbal solicitation signals from more than 200 women at a party for a study.

The repercussions of Monica Moore's discoveries can be seen here, in slipping request. At a party, these are the moves that get men to approach you and talk to you, huntresses. The number that follows each move indicates the number of times Moore observed it succeed in the experiment.21

How Effectively Ladies Take the Principal Action not suggested! 8 Sisters, don't be shy about starting a discussion. Think about it along these lines on the off chance that you really want more fortitude. In order for a woman to select the best partner and ensure the species' survival, female choice is a requirement imposed by evolution. By outrightly attracting Mr. Attractive Outsider, you just satisfy your instinctual predetermination. Nature would appreciate it.

Still reserved? Do you think he will think you are too outgoing if you smile broadly at him in the crowd or "accidentally" brush up against him? He won't because, happily, the male self-image takes precedence.

retroactively. For the next ten minutes, he won't even be aware that he wasn't the one who made the initial overture. Moore's research shows that when women make nonverbal advances to them, men mistakenly think they are making the first move.

I decided to add my own research to Monica Moore's established findings while I was dining alone recently at one of the many TGIF restaurants in Albany, New York. As I finished dinner, I was thinking about the program for the following day's seminar because I had to give a talk to a group of single people the next morning. I organized a section of my discussion called "the grin," in which I would tell women that it means a lot to smile at an attractive man.

I thought to myself, "Leil, you hypocrite." When you don't even have the nerve to smile at strangers, you won't tell women tomorrow morning to smile bravely." A handsome man was reading as he finished his dinner a few tables away from me while I was pondering this. I mused, "OK, Leil, courage." Give it a try! As a result, I smiled at the attractive stranger.

The unfortunate individual dived once more into his book with astonished eyes and a confused expression. Soon after, he once more looked up. I continued to smile. Once more his nose evaporated in his figuring out material. A few minutes later, the handsome stranger got up and went to the men's room, passing my table. As he passed by, I had to force myself to smile once more. The baffled individual pushed on, wracking his head in the process.

Things got interesting after that. When he got back from the men's room, he walked slowly by my table. As I gave him a second look up at me, I smiled. Mr. More unusual's strolling halted. It checked out to start visiting as though we had been formally presented after I had suffocated him in grins. At my table, he joined me for coffee.

Page 52 Well, I invited this Sam to my morning seminar, and he showed up. I told the crowd, normally without uncovering Sam's character, the narrative of how my grin had coordinated a gathering with the solitary cafe to show the "grin" part of my class.

"You know, Leil, I suppose you were examining me in that little story you told," Sam said after the class. Despite this, he continued, "I thought it was I who made the approach to you," giving the impression of being completely perplexed but actually being quite sincere. Sam, yes.

Sisters, I should illuminate you that the male inner self is a surprising peculiarity. He will neglect to recollect that you didn't make the essential procedure if you set out to smile thoroughly, motion, feature a seat, and welcome him to sit — or pick basically any of Monica Moore's strategies.

The eighth method for trackers is:

Right when you spot a likely Quarry, huntresses, don't keep things under control for him to approach. ACT FIRST. Essentially, you need to act first. Utilize any of the dependable strategies. It is pretty much as close as you can get to jabbing him in the bum with a needle loaded up with PEA.

Page 53: Your Underlying Developments: Permit Your Body To talk Science shows that the two assistants' underlying non-verbal correspondence chooses if they will turn out to be horrendously enchanted. Quite possibly of the most committed scientist working in the lab of affection was Dr. Timothy Perper. He spent different thousand exhausting hours perched on the stools of singles' bars and focusing on men, women, and their underlying sentiment moves.

In his singles' bar lab, Dr. Perper, like experts focusing on hamster mating plans, again and again saw a comparable illustration of sentiment. As people picked each other up, he stayed ardent at his post, composing notes, making graphs, and making forecasts about equations. In the best logical practice, the non-verbal communication example of couples getting to know one another was then separated into five quite certain means.

As demonstrated by Dr. Perper's disclosures, the couple ended up leaving together or heading out to have a great time when the two assistants adhered to a specific progression of exercises. Notwithstanding, regardless of whether neither one of the accomplices broke the grouping coincidentally, the couple floated separated.

Many individuals searching for affection take social moving illustrations with expectations of meeting a possible accomplice. They put a lot of effort into learning the fox trot, waltz, cha-cha, rhumba, and cha-cha. In any case, in the main dance, which the shrewd specialist named the Dance of Closeness, they crash and burn with a vengeance.

What occurs during the Dance of Closeness? They are just as new and well-organized as the Tennessee Three step dances. These are the successive moves you want to initiate if you have any desire to draw near to your PLP. On the off chance that you overlook any of the accompanying five inward psyche nonverbal correspondence steps, your Quarry will lose interest and meander once again into the singles' wild. Accordingly, you ought to focus on all of them.

The Personal Dance's Underlying Step: Nonverbal Correspondence Once the two accomplices are inside talking range, one of them will grin, gesture, or take a gander at the other, as depicted in the first part, to show their presence.

Second Step: After that, one of the two speaks. The person in question might say something or ask. Even just a brief "Hello!" got it, however there is a trade of words.

Third Activity: Turning now, it becomes intriguing. At the point when one accomplice tosses out the verbal sign, the beneficiary ought to promptly answer by turning their head essentially toward the speaker. Yet again the Tracker seldom endeavors in the event that the person being referred to doesn't.

Then again, they begin talking assuming the accomplice turns heartily toward the speaker. A critical turn happens after that. Hunter and Quarry gradually shift from simply pointing in the same direction to using their shoulders. In the event that they like one another, their middles promptly turn, and their knees follow.

Their whole bodies ultimately go up against each other in useful social occasions.

The straight-on, knees-to-knees, midriff to-stomach, ceaseless course of action can require minutes to hours.

With each increas-

ing turn, closeness increments. With each dismiss, closeness diminishes.

Fourth Activity: A strong love mixture, contact, compares with conversing with each other and bit by bit moving in a similar heading. He gives you a pretzel and a light hand brush. She tenderly eliminates some build up from your coat. The touch is transitory and practically elusive.

How you answer their most imperative touch is a critical figure whether the correspondence proceeds.

When you slightly stiffen your shoulders while your partner brushes your jacket, he or she may subconsciously and frequently incorrectly interpret this as rejection. Regardless, it is too far to turn back.

Dr. Perper illuminates us that it is turning out to be progressively hard to recognize Quarry and Tracker right now in the development. Once the underlying touch has been performed, the couple is on their way to becoming a couple for the majority of the night after getting well and, surprisingly, returning.

A further inconsistency happens close to this time. Eye-to-eye to eye connection suggests an alternate character.

In 1977, a specialist saw that couples visually connected when they looked as opposed to visually connecting. This is the visual excursion we recently examined as their eyes gradually center around developments surrounding each other's countenances, hair, necks, shoulders, and torsos22.

Fiveth Stage: The most enchanting piece of synchronization is watching the last step. The couple begins to move in time with one another, as if to demonstrate their newly discovered love for one another.

The man and woman, for instance, might both reach for their beverages and return their glasses to the table at the same time. They then continue to intentionally move their weight together, influence to the music together, knock some people's socks off together toward a break from an external perspective, and afterward at the same time glance back at each other.

"Once synchronized, couples can stay in synchronicity obviously perpetually until the bar closes, until they finish dinner and refreshments and ought to leave, until their train comes to any place it is going," Dr. Perper created on page 56. to put it another way, until something from the outside gets in the way and makes it impossible for them to talk to each other. 23 In any case, Timothy Perper and his exploration accomplices knew that if either accomplice staggered on even one of the first five stages, for example, not getting in a state of harmony with different, they could begin singing the couple's last curtain call.

As of late, I had the joy of watching a couple who appeared to be profoundly enamored. I was eating with a young couple at a bar-standing up to table in a diner. Their bodies were

totally confronting one another, and they were inclining in the direction of one another, fundamentally tumbling off their

stools. They generally grinned and gestured as they murmured pieces of discussion. Their movements were completely synchronized as they returned their glasses to the bar, occasionally rubbing their hands against one another. They shared a laugh. They traded glares. They took a gander at each other without jumping predictably, with the exception of when outside upheaval went after their classified space. They took certain individuals' breath away and looked back at each other as one even by then. It would be said that people are charmed.

The server saw me noticing the couple as I covered my bill. She replied, "Better accept it, I've been watching them, too," smiling widely. Is it true or not that they are valuable?

Indeed, I agreed. They have all the earmarks of being enamored profoundly."

She said, "Goodness, no. " Just ten minutes ago, they met!"

I contemplated that they should have both perused Perper's Standards. On the other hand, they were "jes' doing a what comes natch-ur-lee!" as Annie

Oakley shows in her film Annie Get Your Weapon.

In When You Are Quarry, two accomplices are expected for the Dance of Closeness. You ought to recall the means regardless, when you are Quarry. Unfortunately, numerous likely associations on Page 57 don't work out immediately on the grounds that, unintentionally, the Quarry repulses the Tracker through nonverbal correspondence.

As opposed to deer and bear trackers, human trackers and huntresses are beset with an infection. It's known as weakness or timidity. You ought to show that you are willing Quarry and a good lover in the Dance of Closeness when a Tracker or Huntress checks you out.

Diana, my darling, and I once hit up a party together. As the alluring man grinned at Diana, she dismissed. She told me, "That attractive man around there grinned at me."

I answered, "Superb." Yet again smile.

The individual started to rapidly stay near us. Diana as of late kept on speaking with me, and I don't know whether it was humility or a desire to keep things quiet that made her not smile at him. A couple of moments later, we saw the appealing outsider speaking heartily with another lady. Diana was snuffed out. " Goodness, I deduce he saw me close up and decided not to chat with me," she told me.

I needed to shake her when I said, "No, Diana." It was only that you didn't answer his advances. She ought to have moved in the direction of him in the central dance of sweethearts to show that she was open.

Everywhere, chances of this sort are much of the time missed. Quarry a significant part of the time yells out for get, promptly transforming into the individual who moved away.

The Word That Could Save Your Relationship As you banter with your new Quarry, you arrive at the place of understanding that: This individual is truly great.

It's something beyond actual fascination. This individual has the ability to foster connections." Following thirty seconds, your heart begins to pulsate a little quicker and your throat unexpectedly becomes dry. Is this the start of something critical?

Your frontal cortex unexpectedly starts Page 58 considering the impression you're making on your Quarry as opposed to mission control directing all of your body parts to make the brilliant moves. Breathing becomes shallow. You sense a tendency to choke out of shock. Sadly, that is a result of PEA entering your cerebrum.

Watch out! You will not be really captivating and charming assuming tension sets in and you begin to stress over each move. Zeroing in on Perper's Guidelines and trying to audit whether contact goes before synchronicity are at present unthinkable. Or then again, on the other hand, was it going before contact? During seasons of high nervousness like these, you want a basic method for getting your body to do what Dr. Perper instructs you to do so you can focus on what your great new Quarry is talking about.

Made in the USA
Monee, IL
18 December 2024

74258443R00069